No Fishing in My Pond
a Blueprint to Protect Your Sales

Rick Rivers

First published in 2011
Revised and re-published in 2018

ISBN-13: 978-1721081646
ISBN-10: 172108164X

LCCN#: 2010915018

Printed in the United States of America

This book is dedicated to all the hard-working small business owners I know and have worked with over the years. Owning a small business is one of the greatest challenges that anyone can ever have. You must wear many hats and be able to switch them at a moment's notice. A small business owner might have to go from customer service representative to janitor to mediator in the same hour. Owning your own business can have great rewards and will truly shape who you are as a business person. Small business owners need to seek the help that they need in order to survive.

I would also like to thank my new friends at Flowerchat.com. This chat room gave me much inspiration while finishing this book and for my next book. The stories, both good and bad, showed me again just how important it is for small business owners to have a support system. Small business ownership or entrepreneurism can be a lonely place but with a chat room like this you're never alone. Thanks to all the thousands on Flowerchat.com.

I would like to thank my wife, Susie, and my children, Jessica and Jason. They, along with my extended church family, are always there to support and encourage me in all my endeavors. For this I am blessed.

Contents

Foreword
by Keith Cameron Smith

Some people are students of financial success. Students of financial success don't have to study very long before they start understanding the importance of marketing. Once a student of financial success begins to understand the power and importance of marketing he becomes a student of marketing. Graduating from a student of financial success to a student of marketing is like graduating from college and moving into the real world of entrepreneurship.

This is a great little book because Rick Rivers was once a student of financial success but became a serious student of marketing. By saying he is a serious student of marketing I mean he applies what he learns in his own business and reaps the benefits. Studying a subject is great but application is even better. This book is written from the perspective of someone who has studied and applied what he has learned and figured out what works and what doesn't. There are a lot of theories about success and marketing, but this book gives you more than just theories. It gives you specialized knowledge— which is more powerful and valuable than generalized knowledge.

Marketing is a subject that you must become a student of if you want to learn how to consistently earn profits. The insights you will gain from this little book can make a big difference in your bottom line. Read this book more than once and let Rick teach you what he has learned so that the money you have earned next year is a lot more than what you earned last year.

Keith Cameron Smith, Author
The Top 10 Distinctions between Millionaires and the Middle Class

Chapter 1
The Pond

The inspiration for this book comes from a favorite pastime my wife and I like to do. We love to get out of the house and just drive or "putz" around town and even the next few cities over. It's a fun thing that we like to do together. We ride around all the different neighborhoods looking at nice homes, landscaping, etc. We especially love to ride through the gated communities in our area. We wait until the right moment and "get in" somehow to check them out.

One day while riding through one of those gated communities, I noticed that all the retention ponds had signs in them. The signs read: "No fishing here, residents only." Suddenly, it dawned on me that MY pond, which is full of my customers, was wide open to be fished in. I got very nervous that I had no sign up to protect my pond and I knew that it was time to take measures to protect it.

Business owners need to "fence in their ponds" to keep their competitors out. So many business owners don't believe they have to protect their most valuable assets; their customers. By posting a sign, they have protected something that they feel is so valuable to the residents that it warranted signage. The sign simply but clearly states what they mean: I want to protect my customers so badly that I decided to build a fence around my pond. This will send a clear message to all, "no fishing allowed."

Now, by just putting up the sign you won't stop people from fishing or attempting to fish in your pond. The biggest challenge for small-business owners is to keep their customers coming back and keep them enthused about the product and company. Every company has a pond; some are just bigger than others and have more fish in them.

The pond is stocked with customers who like you, your product, and your price. They don't have a problem paying the price that you charge, or they wouldn't be there. I'm amazed at how easily customers can be stolen or lured away from my competitors with a simple thank you or discount. I very rarely stole or lured a customer because my price was cheaper. It was 90% service. We simply offered a better service plan than the competitors in my area.

I observed a number of businesses in researching for this book. As part of my observation, I would look around and see if I could first determine the pond and if it was protected. I found that over 80% of small businesses that I visited had no sign. Their pond was wide open for anyone to fish in and there are plenty of "good fishermen" out there. Some of the businesses had the hardware to build the sign but just never finished it.

I also walked into some businesses that you could tell had numerous signs up all over. They had programs in place to protect their customer base and also to encourage the customer base to come back and spend

> *The pond is stocked with customers who like you, your product, and your price.*

more. So many businesses focus on the new customer but if you're doing your job right then your existing customers will bring you new customers on a silver platter. The sole job of a small-business owner is to get customers to buy more and spend more with you.

Let's pause here for a minute and make sure everybody is up to speed with what I am talking about. First, you must understand what your "pond" is and who is potentially in it. If you are in the floral industry like me, then your pond consists of everyone who buys flowers and related items on a semi-consistent basis.

There is quite a bit to contend with nowadays in the floral industry. Not only do I have to protect my pond from my competitors, but I also have to think about online drop ship sales, grocery stores, wholesale warehouses, and even some of the wire services that are supposed to be helping me grow my business. All of these have the potential to yank the fish right out from under my nose if I don't protect my pond properly.

I don't think you need to be overly concerned and stay up nights thinking about the scavengers who might be raiding your pond while you sleep. If you are doing a few basic things right (things we will cover in this book) then your pond has all the fence you need to keep those sneaky critters out and all of your fish safe and happy.

Many of you are no doubt asking how you stock the pond and keep it full of customers? The answer is that it takes hard work, spending a significant amount of time on marketing, and developing systems that will help you manage your marketing plan and keep it on course.

One of the greatest things that small-business owners fail to recognize is that when a customer calls or walks into your place of business they have already made a decision to buy from you. In my store that ratio is 85% to 90%. All I have to do is be a great "closer." By "closer" I mostly mean JUST DON'T BLOW IT. They are there to buy so get out of their way!

Many businesses are more geared towards

price (but remember only 13% of America buys by price or has to by price). That means that 87% of the buying population is wide open to buy your product at YOUR price. So, the fact that you are a little higher in price really doesn't matter to them. More on this later.

Now, let's take a look into your pond. First, look in your database and see how many names, addresses, email or phone numbers you have. Your database should contain all the people that have been doing business with you in the last three years at least. Some marketing professionals say that your records need five to seven years of customers, but I like the three-year method of existing customers.

If you don't have a database whereby you can collect and keep information, for Pete's sake, get one! You need to have customer information at your fingertips at all times in order to be able to do business with any level of competency. I meet business owners who think they have all the information that they need stored right in their heads. These, of course, are the same people who can't ever find their glasses that are usually resting on top of the same head that contains all this information.

After you get your customers segmented into a list, divide the list into three groups. Group one contains those who have bought more than five times in the last calendar year. Group two includes those who bought less than five times in the last two years. The third group is made up of those with no purchases in two years or more.

87% of the buying population is wide open to buy your product at YOUR price.

The first list is what I call your "at risk" list. These are the people who like what you do and clearly enjoy patronizing your store. But, these people are the ones that can be "fished out" the fastest. Perhaps that sounds confusing but think about this: someone who uses your type of service this frequently is always looking for others who offer the same services and products. If your competitors are smart, they will throw a line in your pond and "hook" some of your best customers. One day you will wake up and say, "Who has been fishing in my pond?" It will be at this point that you realize that marketing has been absent from your business plan.

The next list is the customers who are not loyal to you or any other business. They simply float around based on the product and demand and not really price.

They use print media to order and usually go down the list until the questions they want answered get answered and then they buy. They never remember who they bought from or where to go back to if they did like the product and service.

> *You need to be able to say why you are better than your competitors in three sentences or less.*

The last list is the people who have been fished out of your pond or who jumped out of your pond for whatever reason. You need to market all of the lists but in different ways.

The first thing you need to do is to put up a fence all the way around your pond; so, go make a sign and put it up outside your pond. It probably wouldn't hurt to make a real sign and put it somewhere in your store. When the employees ask about the sign it would be a good time to educate them on the importance of the LCV (lifetime client value) of all your customers. When your customers see this sign and inquire, they will feel very appreciated knowing that they are important to you.

Your fence is built with material that you need to be familiar with and use on a regular and consistent basis. First, you need fence posts. The fence posts are your quality product. There is no replacing quality as a foundation to build your business on. If your customer gets a shoddy product from you and you don't make it right happily and immediately, the rest of your fence doesn't matter. No one will have to fish for them. They will find a new pond on their own.

The cross members of your fence are the level of excellent service that you provide. This is the strength behind the structure; without it, the next stiff breeze will blow your fence over. If you are to have success in business, you must commit to excellence in customer service. Florists in particular have very few advantages in the marketplace, but one advantage that we DO have is that we are there when we are needed most. The relationships that you build with your customers and community will carry you when other businesses are failing.

There is no replacing quality as a foundation to build your business on.

If you want to keep anyone out with your fence, you have to have slats, right? The fence slats are your marketing efforts. Whatever means you use to market your business and to get the word out as to why you are better and different, you HAVE to be clear, consistent, and compelling. You need to be able to say why you are better than your competitors in three sentences or less. We live in a short-attention-span society, so you have to be able to cut to the chase with your message. Ask yourself "why am I better?" If you don't know, you better find out. If you do know, you better be able to articulate it.

Your marketing has to be consistent in order to have any real success. When people think of flowers in Ormond Beach, Florida, they think of Rick and A Floral Boutique. This is because we have stayed in front of our customers, community, and have been consistent over a long period of time. If you do a little marketing, drop off the earth for months, and then try to pick it back up, you have essentially wasted your previous efforts and are now starting from scratch. Consistency is key.

Of the three C's I just gave you (customers, community, consistency), perhaps the most important is that your message MUST be compelling to your customer. Simply put, whatever you do, DON'T BE BORING. I have used everything from a letter to my deceased mom to Rick Rivers, Doctor of Love, to get my customers' attention. I might not write like Hemingway, but at least I ain't boring in my marketing copy. They may not buy from me, but they will remember what I said.

Now that you've fenced in your customers, you have to be able to deliver the level of service and quality products that will keep them coming back and spending the time and money that it takes to keep you on their minds.

LIST ONE

Start an immediate campaign of rewards, thank you, or a value system so that they will feel appreciated for the level of business that they give you. If they are a top 50 customer, tell them and say thank you when telling them. That alone will be enough to keep them coming back.

I recommend at least a three-step marketing program for this list and that you keep a document file for all the campaigns that you run. This is for two reasons: so that you can track the return and so you will not repeat the same campaign. In some cases, however, it is fine to repeat campaigns. I do a "Favorite Mom" campaign every Mother's Day and it still gets great results.

LIST TWO

Begin a marketing campaign by saying "We've missed you." This will let the customers know that you know they've not been around. You are fishing in a pond where they are in an attempt to get them back. Don't be afraid to offer them something crazy. Try to partner with a local restaurant or other vendor with something very enticing to get them back. I partner with local restaurants all the time. I let the owners know what I'm doing and find them typically very willing to chip in.

Let's face it, if I give a customer a free Outback bloom card it's a winning scenario for everyone involved. The customer feels very appreciated (even though he's been in someone else's pond because you were too "lazy" to do some marketing) and Outback gets a new or very appreciative repeat customer.

If you are Outback Steakhouse, this is a smart move. If that customer is a new customer to the Outback chain, then that customer cost Outback less than $2 to get them in the door. It would cost Outback much more than $2 to market that customer from scratch. You see, the Outback would not have known which pond this customer was in. They would have had to mass mail/ mass market a large zip code population (throw a very big expensive net) in order to get the same results. So, I handed Outback a new customer or a repeat customer who just received "value appreciation." If the service and product are up to par and Outback is doing its job, that "free bloom customer" will be back. My local Outback has a young and very aggressive proprietor and he's not afraid to chip in his share. I have several other restaurants in the area that I market with as well.

LIST THREE

This is the hardest and most costly list to market. This list is full of customers who forgot about you, were unhappy with the product or service, moved away, got caught in another net, or just plain don't want to do business with you for whatever reason. You do not want to spend a lot of money on this list, but there are some good customers lying on the bottom of the pond in this list.

When you fish this list, you have to fish at the

top, middle, and bottom of the pond. Your campaign needs to reference the last event in which they bought and be in a survey format so that you can find out why they no longer buy from you. Some will return with an answer and you will be able to sort out the list and discard ones that are no longer relevant.

I would market this list in three ways: first with a survey, as I mentioned; a follow-up with a big reward/ discount offer; and a final attempt close to the "event date" of their last order. A husband might have sent his wife flowers five years ago for the anniversary and now he's divorced. There is still a chance of getting him back (perhaps for the new wife) and your last attempt will win him back.

Never discard a name on any list unless the probability of them purchasing from you is almost zero. Put list three into an archive file and from time to time you have a list to fish from. I only remove names from a list for divorce, death, and dehydration (I'm tired of marketing this person).

Once you have segmented the list and have started your mailings, be satisfied that good is good enough. You have to have a place to start, and if you don't start you will never finish. Once you see results, a pattern will emerge as to buying habits. Although every business has particular buying habits that apply specifically to that business, you will soon find that buying habits are pretty similar across the board. Remember, your lists are the key to success and profits.

Chapter 2
Stocking the Pond

There are many ways that the pond can be stocked, so I'm going to list and go over my favorite ones that have shown great results.

Once someone buys from your store, you need to stay in touch with that customer. Research shows that you need twenty-six touches a year to keep your customer safely in your pond. If you don't stay connected, there's a hole in your fence and one day you may find someone pulling a really big fish out of your pond.

You might be cringing right know thinking you're going to have to spend thousands of dollars to safeguard your pond, but that simply is not the case. Touches   can be through print media, letters, email marketing, social networking sites, robo-calls, personal phone calls, reminder postcards, giveaways, contests, radio talk shows, and the list goes on.

I run at least one campaign per month that involves the entire customer base. I then run separate campaigns for the Top 50, Top 100, or Top 250 customer lists. I believe that you have to tell the customer that you are successful because they are a top customer. You can never say thank you too much.

Every quarter I sort lists from the database for a Top 25, Top 50, and Top 100 list and I take the time to study them. Most names don't move around much, but every now and then a new name will emerge to my surprise. Having a business as large as mine I can't see everything, although I try.

This list also shows how your staff is performing. If they are doing a great job then the lists stay intact with names climbing, not sinking, on the list. When names start to drop down, that's the time to take action before they fall off your list. Once they fall off the list it's harder to get them back on the list, especially if they've left for bad reasons.

The list should clearly show you all the spending habits and the frequency of the purchases. If a name starts to fall and you see that their spending habits have drastically changed, something is wrong. I will call and simply say, "Mrs. Smith, I see you have not purchased from us during the last quarter and normally you're in the Top ___." If you have a decent relationship with your customers, they will tell you everything you want to know. They might have dropped for unforeseen economic conditions, job loss, voluntary cutbacks, etc. The reasons are endless as to why customers are not buying from you anymore. If the report is bad, then while you have Mrs. Smith on the phone you can deal with it. I have rescued many customers by just listening to them and being willing to take corrective action.

Corrective action might mean offering a free service for a later date, refunding a portion of the "bad experience," or simply writing a note of apology. I've seen many good customers slip through the fence because an owner was too proud to say, "I'm sorry" or "we were wrong." My experience has been that customers are very forgiving, and once good service and high-quality product is restored, they are happy.

Before you stock your pond, you must first go fishing. Now, let's discuss ways to catch customers.

VALUE REWARDS SYSTEMS

This is usually a printed item or a punch card that would allow the customer to receive either a discount or a free item after a fixed number of purchases. Some businesses also use a value system that is based on dollars spent. In my retail store, I give discounts once "spending platforms" have been reached. When a customer's account reaches a certain pre-determined spending level, discounts start to apply.

REMINDER SERVICES

In my business, I have one direct mail piece that serves as a reminder that has a 29% return rate. I tell every florist that I meet about it. Most just shrug their shoulders and say, "I tried something like that and it didn't work."

In my career, I have tried many things that haven't worked, and I have found that it is often because of a lack of planning and research. No plan will work unless you study and master what you are doing. This one works because I have spent the time to research and carefully plan for the results I am receiving.

For reminder services to be really successful, you have to use a technique I call "out of time marketing." This means your reminder message has to meet a need and be received at the moment the need is felt the strongest—right before the customer is "out of time."

Before you stock your pond, you must first go fishing.

It is a waste of time, for example, to remind someone of an anniversary or birthday a month before the date. We tested mail systems and make our mail piece get to the customer two days prior to the event. The envelope reads "Special event information" or "special occasion" and it gets opened at an alarming rate. We had one month that hit 29% and if you know anything about direct mail, the average is 1% to 3%. Men and women do respond differently to marketing techniques and they have to be adjusted at times to meet the unique needs.

EMAIL MARKETING

We have about 1,500 names in our email marketing list. Some people say that they have thousands, but we only count the people who are proven buyers for our business. We use our email list as a follow-up and reminder tool, with an email the afternoon before or the morning of an event. For our male customers, the response rate is in the high 70% range. For women, it is considerably less. Our female customers are always appreciative of the email reminder, but do not tend to buy as often as men because of it.

If you have been in business for any length of time you probably are already well aware of the differences between the buying patterns of men and women. By and large, you can count on women being planned buyers. In other words, they know well ahead of time that they are going to buy flowers for a certain occasion and even what kind of flowers they

If [email] comes at just the right time and says the right thing, it is very effective.

might buy.

Men, by contrast, tend to be impulse buyers. If they happen to pass your store and some kind of external stimulus produces the thought "Hey, maybe I better get some flowers" then they will pull into your store and buy the thing that looks best at the moment. The stereotype doesn't hold true across the board of course, but you might be surprised how often this is exactly the case.

I have a friend who used to buy flowers for his wife every Friday on his way home from work. He passed a roadside flower vendor on the way home. He would see the guy sitting on his five-gallon paint bucket selling flowers and it would remind him to stop and get some. He no longer buys his wife flowers every Friday. Why? The roadside vendor moved to the other side of the road. It would now require a U-turn. No can do.

Emails can be like a roadside vendor for you. They can remind the right demographic of your customer base to buy from you. If it comes at just the right time and says the right thing, it is very effective. Use it wisely.

ROBO CALLS

Some industries have been using this type of marketing successfully for years. There are several companies out there that will provide you with this service. You will give them your database and they will pre-record your message and send them out to your customers. I get these calls often from people that I buy from and I always listen to them.

Identifying yourself at the beginning of the message is crucial if you don't want people to hang up on you. I start mine off with "Hi, this is Rick Rivers, your florist" and then give the message to them. The message must include a code for tracking so when they call, and you ask, "How did you hear about us?" they can say, "I received a message from Rick." This allows you to measure your marketing efforts.

Robo calling, like any other marketing tool, requires planning and courtesy. If you set your calls to go out during the busiest time of the day, you annoy people and burn your credibility as a marketer. I know at least one business that set its robo-calls to go out at 2:00 p.m. but accidentally set it for 2:00 a.m. You can imagine the rest of that story.

POSTCARDS

I like postcards for marketing holidays and special events. A lot of times I will prepare a campaign and do all the work months in advance and have them ready and waiting to mail. Once a customer buys from us they are in a "targeted" list related to buying habits or time of purchase. A lot of businesses, for example, have customers that only buy during certain times of the year. The business owner should know that through his preparation. Customers are very easy to figure out and then target. We use postcards on these targeted lists, too.

If you are going to use postcards, I advise using the larger size, or preferably the odd size. The point of any mailing is to get the piece read by the customer. If you send a tiny postcard you are far more likely to have it lost in a pile of mail or thrown away as junk. If your card is large or an odd size, it stands out and can't be sorted into a pile. This gives you at least a small advantage and helps get your piece looked at, read, and hopefully responded to.

DIRECTIONAL ADVERTISING

The car and home sale industries having been using this for years. This is where one or more people are employed to stand on the street corner with signage that directs passersby to a business. The wording on the sign is the key to any success here. Obviously, with too many words the sign becomes unreadable. The copy on the sign should say the one thing that you most want to convey. The more clever the copy, the better the response will be.

PRICE PERFORMANCE

Every shopper likes a good "loss leader item." The purpose of a loss leader is to get customers in to buy the loss leader and then entice them to also purchase something else. Research shows that the rate of additional purchase is high. You also now have the opportunity to gather information and put them into a general list for marketing. If they become customers of your store, then you've added a customer at a very low "new customer acquisition" cost. The price of the loss leader covered the cost of acquiring the customer, so you made a little money on the additional items they bought and got someone new in your store.

WARM CALLS

Everyone has no doubt heard the expression "cold calling." This must be the most annoying of all forms of marketing. I would never even consider using this method at all! The only reason I even mention it is because I've turned this phrase around to call it "warm calls." Customers love when you call after they've used you and ask for their feedback. I have had some very pleasant experiences using this method.

Warm calls produce good relationships ...

I remember one call in particular, several years ago. An elderly gentleman came into the store to send several orders out of town. I called two weeks later and introduced myself and asked him how his experience was. After listening to him tell me how pleased everyone was with their flowers, I went in for the kill— "How did you get to us?" I asked. As it turns out, his neighbor had received a letter in the mail at the passing of a loved one and she passed it along to her neighbor. In the course of our conversation, I found out this gentleman was a former professional basketball player and college star from the late 1930s. He was eighty years old but still had the memories and wanted to share them. Now, every time he calls the store, he asks the clerk to say hello to Rick. Warm calls produce good relationships and good relationships are good for business.

RADIO SHOW

Last year I started my own radio show. My friend and I began the radio show to highlight local businesses and discuss business-related topics. We started with one show per week and still have the same hour today. We have sponsors that pay for the ad times and we both get to promote our businesses several times during the hour. Thousands of people listen to this station and the demographics are an older listening audience. I've built many relationships because of the show and lots of folks stop by the store just to discuss what they heard us say on the radio.

Chapter 3
The Counter

Several days a week I like to go out for breakfast and join the guys for coffee. About two years ago, I added another café to my arsenal. This new café has a long counter with seating for six people. When I came in, the third seat from the end was open and so I grabbed that one. Every time I came in it seemed that the same seat was open. The regulars sat in the same seat each day and had for years, so I guess seat #3 was mine for the taking.

This chapter is about what can be learned by the people you sit and eat with. We are in such a busy life cycle that there is no time left for just sitting and listening to other business people go through "business life" worrying about payroll, vendors, and accounts receivable. Many are passing up on the great opportunities that are right under their noses—or their forks.

This counter was filled with years of experience from retired military, business leaders, city employees, etc. So many life experiences and just many years of wisdom sat at this counter, over

100 years when totaled. All the people who sat at the counter were very intuitive as to the surroundings and the pulse of the community. I listened when they spoke and often learned much when I did.

Later, several other people would join us at the counter and seats would become like "breakfast idol." People would roll in, sit down, and stay a spell. I think people like these "breakfast holes" because of the conversation. Even the owner and the server added to the conversation, with their life experiences and observations. They both had numerous jobs within their industry and had great stories to share. The owner had come from a corporate big box restaurant and her experience was based on what she had been taught. She brought her experiences to her restaurant and adapted it to make it her own style. A lot of what she brought in worked and some did not. The main server had her own style of serving customers and was very good at what she did. When people put their hearts into their jobs, it shows.

You can learn so much from using your two ears, especially in the business world. My favorite Bible verse is located in the book of Proverbs and says: "there is wisdom in counsel." I believe in that verse with my whole heart. Because of it, I have learned not to let time force my decisions, but instead to rely on wise counsel and facts. (This was not always the case for me.) I am sometimes accused of being too slow to make a decision, but I always run things past my wife and others. I've received some of the best advice from the people that I sit and eat with.

Perhaps you are asking what this has to do with marketing. Marketing is the art of listening to the people who buy your products or services and then applying what they want into your business plan. If this is done right, the profit rolls in. If it is done poorly, expect loss to follow. The difference between profit and loss can be as simple as one bad decision.

Many people go into business thinking they know it all and refuse to be taught by others. I thought I knew it all for nearly twenty years, until I finally met my match. I finally allowed someone to teach me what marketing and customer service really is.

> *Marketing is the art of listening to the people who buy your products...*

Customer service is like making love to a gorilla. You don't quit when you're satisfied, you quit when the gorilla is satisfied. For years I had this sign up in my back room and every new employee would stand and read the sign and then look at me bewildered. I would explain to them that this concept is better caught than taught. You have to learn from people who have been there, people who have lost or made money and made all the decisions, good or bad. Then, and only then, will you learn. You will hear the excitement in people's voices if they made money or the bitter anguish if they lost. Once you lose, or if you're losing as we speak, you will give marketing another look.

Another concept of this chapter is self-education. For years I would only read items that pertained to my industry because I had been brainwashed to read or learn only things that pertained to the floral business. I was told that our business was different and so we had to all look and quack the same. After twenty years of quacking like everyone else, I finally figured out that the only people getting rich were the people who were telling me how to quack!

I belong to a national marketing group called, Glazer, Kennedy, Insiders Circle. This group has thousands of members and meets twice year. We sit around in large and small groups teaching each other what is working for today's marketers. Every business owner should have a plan that fits into their business model. These meetings are the reason why I'm still growing. That is why I told you that you should NOT quack like everyone else and that my business was really no different than any other business. Yes, we do things a little different in the flower business but overall, all businesses are alike. Sales plus service equals profits!

So, I began to spend time each week working ON my business and not just working IN my business. You will be surprised what you will learn about your competitors and the industry that you are in if you will just take the time to do some research and see for yourself. If you don't take the time for self-education and speak to the people who use your products, you are leaving a lot of money on the table. I used to look at the customer who wanted to share with me as time that I didn't have. But now I welcome it and at the end of the sharing I always learn something about the customer, their family, or their buying habits. So, when I sit at my breakfast or lunch place and I talk to the people who surround me, the information that I get from them is invaluable to the ongoing success of my business and the marketing edge that I maintain.

I spend a lot of money to attend my national marketing group, various seminars, and industry events for the purpose of learning. I always try to return to my place of business and implement what I have learned. Otherwise, I'm just wasting my family's money. I got tired of hearing "my business is different" and decided to make a change and encourage others to do the same.

All businesses are alike; they may just get to the sale in a little different way. All businesses need a customer who will buy again and again, and have that customer refer a new customer. At that point, the cycle can begin again. During the above process, the business needs a plan to keep the cycle going.

This sounds easy, but it is one of the hardest things that I've ever had to do. I know I'm not alone, because in my industry 65% of florists are losing money or just breaking even. If that doesn't scare you, I don't know what will.

Very few business owners look at the profit side of business. Some do a good job at the initial sale, but then go back to sleep. When someone goes out of business, I ask them, "What do you think the problem was?" I usually know the answer but rarely hear it from the out-of-business owner. They typically blame everybody from their mom and dad in their childhood years to the employee with the least amount of responsibilities. When a business fails, it is usually the owner's fault. They failed to maintain cost, maintain sales, or have proper systems in place to monitor the function of their business. I am amazed, especially in the restaurant industry, at how an owner will outfit a restaurant and spend thousands of dollars to open, but then not have enough working capital to carry the business past a few months. A majority of businesses fail in the first year, and it is for similar reasons. They lack the planning and funding to carry out their goal.

When I get survey cards in the mail, I know that the business has an owner who cares about the dollars that I spend in his business and he will continue to be a leader in his industry. It's time for you to find out what your customers expect from you and then see that you are living up to their expectations.

One of the hardest lessons I ever learned in business was after getting back the results of my first survey card. I asked people to rate me and then tell me something that we were doing wrong. After mailing about 300 cards to the top customers, forty responded and over half mentioned that we weren't open early enough. As the owner, I assumed being open 9:00 a.m. to 5:00 p.m. was what we needed to do. I observed that other florists were open during these same hours, and just made the assumption that it was right for me, too. One good customer stated, "I go to work at 8:00 a.m. and you're never open."

I decided after the input that we would change our hours. We began to open at 8:00 a.m. and close at 5:30p.m. We began to see our sales increase and now 8:00 to 9:00 a.m. is the second busiest hour of the day for us. You have to talk to your customers and find out their needs, then adapt to what they want. You might be inconvenienced a little, but that is life!

The value of listening can never be

overstated. Those who do not welcome customer complaints are doomed to make the same mistakes over and over and to lose customers for avoidable reasons.

There are ample ways to listen to your customers, and many of them are even free of charge. Social media offers the greatest opportunity in the history of business to eavesdrop on your customers, to find out what they really think and feel, and to discover what they value. You should be using social media to connect with your customers in a personal way, and to really listen to what they are saying, both to you and to one another.

Facebook is an especially good tool simply because it is so widely used. In fact, if Facebook were a country, it would be the fourth most populated country in the world. Facebook provides a great opportunity to do just what I said above, to build relationships with your customers and to LISTEN to what they are saying.

Many business owners are technology or cultural-phenomenon resistant, but in order to really compete in the marketplace, you have to be at least somewhat willing to get on board with things that your customers are on board with. Facebook would be a good example of this. So, for those of you who are lost, let me help you get started. Here are five things you can do today to help your business with Facebook.

CREATE A FACEBOOK PAGE

Your business Facebook page is activity central of your Facebook marketing presence. It is the Houston for your space station. With a Facebook page, Facebook users can "like" your company, product, or promotion. As a Facebook user who "likes" your business, your name and logo will appear on their profile page and your name will appear in their profile feed. This is the lifeblood of your Facebook presence and the place for people to find out about you, what you do, and what you offer.

Consequently, Facebook users will discover your Facebook page through their friends' profiles and through Facebook searches, and your page will grow virally. In other words, you won't have to work for it, it will happen organically as people are exposed to your business.

As a bonus benefit, Fan pages rank very high in search engine results, helping to boost your SEO rankings. Facebook also provides you with some good stats on your page in a weekly email.

UTILIZE FACEBOOK EVENTS

As soon as you have created your Facebook page, you can begin to utilize the Facebook Events feature for promotions you're running. For example, a local flower shop may want to create a promotion for a Fresh Flower Friday. A restaurant may want to promote a weekly happy hour or other in-house event. Essentially, anything that you want people to respond to or attend can be promoted through the Events feature.

When you create an Event, it is automatically promoted on your Facebook page. When Facebook users RSVP to your event (Dave Johnson is attending Happy Hour Friday at Shooters, etc.), their friends see the updates on their profile or news feed. You have the opportunity to have them respond with a yes, a no, or even a maybe, increasing critical interaction between you and your potential customers. To increase the coolness factor about creating Events, consider that even if someone responds with a no or a maybe, the event still goes into their event calendar. So, every time they look at the calendar, your event is in front of them.

CREATE AN INTERACTIVE POLL

One easy way to create a little buzz is to simply get people talking. What better way to get people talking then to ask questions that people care about? You may not care which flower people like better, roses or lilies, or if Audi is better than BMW. But, wherever opinions are involved a buzz is sure to follow and a buzz does a valuable thing for your business—it gets you noticed.

People love to feel as though they are a part of something. They love to see how they compare to others. A simple poll is a great way to get people interacting with you and to become familiar with you and your Facebook site. When they interact with you on a regular basis, they will begin to know you, trust you, and allow you to earn their business.

How to add a poll to your Facebook page:

> From your home page on the left side, click the application link.

> In the search bar, search for Poll application - several will pop up. Pick the one you want.

> Once the application page comes up, click on the Allow link.

> Click on "Click here to get started" and follow the prompts

CONTINUOUSLY ADD FRESH CONTENT

Your Facebook page is not a "set it and forget" deal. It has to be kept fresh in order for anyone to pay attention to you. If you let your content get stale, you will find that people will quickly check out in search of the next most interesting thing.

Consistency in your posting is a major factor in keeping your constituency paying attention. If you become sporadic, you will lose credibility fast. You should be posting daily, or every other day at a minimum. Update your Facebook page with fresh videos, photos, links, and other items of interest.

This is not to say that you need to be a Facebook "nuisance" and post your every waking move. Use your best judgment and, above all, be interesting!

TALK TO YOUR CUSTOMERS

The number one benefit of Facebook for your business is that it affords you the opportunity to build relationships with your current and potential customers. Take advantage of every opportunity to engage your Facebook community. You do this by creating your own content (publishing your posts, etc.), but also by interacting with what THEY are doing.

People love to have feedback on their posts, especially when it is interesting and engaging. You should be paying attention to what your Facebook community is saying and be commenting back every time it is appropriate. This creates a scenario where not only are YOUR friends seeing what you are saying, but you are gaining access to the entire network of the person you are commenting to.

Building relationships, creating credibility, establishing standing in your community—these are the real benefits of Facebook. Join the conversation and reap the rewards.

P.S... Here's a free tip: People love to be recognized on their birthdays and anniversaries. Facebook provides this information for you on all of your Facebook community. Begin to establish rapport by sending a short birthday or anniversary greeting. Make it a habit to check and take the few minutes to post a birthday or anniversary wish. Believe me, it will be well worth your time.

Chapter 4
The Habit, Money, and Sales

This chapter deals with how to determine the buying habits of your customers and the amount of money they will spend with you. I call this the "oh yeah" rule in small business.

For years I had no idea how to determine this or how to take advantage of it. Several years ago, while vacationing in Maine I toured a large florist in Portland who truly had it together. This store had been in business for over 100 years and still was thriving. The employees were upbeat, the store looked amazing, and the image was fresh and alive. I asked the owner what he attributed his success to and without hesitation he said, "I know who I'm talking to and what they want to buy."

This sounds so "common sense" but most small-business owners aren't even familiar with this concept. This owner (family owned) worked six days a week in the business supervised all the main functions and had systems in place for employees to follow. They did at least three surveys a year and on every holiday or buying event they marketed the top 500 customers (spending volume) and kept the business in front of them.

They market their business solely based on dollars and spending habits. They don't get burned out and lose interest in life or the business because they are able to stay ahead of their competitors. I think burnout in most small-business owners is from being behind the eight-ball business wise, not from the actual work. During my twenty-five years I went through this about three times. It seemed like once every seven years I either climbed the mountain or got thrown off of it and had to re-climb it again. During all three times it cost me a lot of money to re-climb the mountain and I was soon tired of wasting money. But once you take charge of your business and get ahead of the curve, burnout is non-existent or at least greatly reduced.

Let's take a look at the buying habits of our customers. Every business should have a way to communicate and document contact with its customer base. If they don't have a way to convey their message or special offers, then they must rely on advertising to do the work for them. The fast-food industry, beer industry, and tobacco industry all rely solely on advertising. They have a large presence in a brand and so they spend thousands in advertising and hope that you (the consumer) will remember and buy their product.

In most small businesses that doesn't work, but many are doing it because that's all they know.

They will let anyone who walks through the door do the promoting for them and pay them handsomely to do it. When it comes to advertising, the buying habits of the person buying from you has not been determined or any thought given to the sales process.

Any small business should have a way to document who the customer is, what they buy, and what they spend. All of the "big boxes" ask for your zip code when you buy, and some go even further and request your phone number.

Small-business owners would be wise to pay attention to and copy what all the big guys are doing and then build upon it. One of my favorites is Office Depot. They always ask for your rewards number which is your phone number. They do this for the sole purpose of tracking your buying habits. They tell you that you are "building points" and discounts but they are really building a pattern of your buying habits.

All of us get Office Depot coupons in the mail and the coupons are usually in our "buying related field." I will call this the BRF for that company. What that means is if you buy certain products from them and your habits remain consistent, they are going to market to you in this field of related items. I don't buy any computer products from Office Depot, so I never get those coupons. All of mine are on printing supplies because that is what I purchase from them.

Many times, businesses spend so much money on marketing people who they have no chance to get a sale from. The main reason is they don't know the habits, so they are trying to throw the "big net" and catch everyone. While writing this chapter I received a coupon in the mail for women's hair products. This item is not in my buying pattern because A) I'm not a woman and B) I have no hair. They evidently bought some sort of list and then did not qualify or clean up the list. They wasted a lot of money marketing to me, and I suspect others like me. They could have at least addressed it to "Resident" so possibly my wife would have picked it up.

I'm amazed at the money wasted in the advertising and marketing world. There are multitudes of people out there making a great living on small-business owners and not offering very much. I can't fault the business owner, they can only do what they know, but I can fault them for not being willing to learn.

I suggest you take a day soon and devote it to "working on your business." Find out who makes up the top 10, 25, 50, and 100 customers of your business. I think it will shock you when you see their buying habits and the dollar amounts. When I first looked at my top 10, I only predicted three names correctly. I was really off in who I thought my top spenders were. Once you have this information, you can determine how to spend, who to spend on, and when to spend. Once you've determined the buying habits of your customers, your job becomes much easier.

After you've determined the buying habits and frequency of buying you can begin to look at the money side of the equation. If I haven't told you already, less than 10% of the buying population makes purchasing decisions solely based on price. The actual facts are that 7% have to buy by price because they are the fixed-income people, single parents and other low-income earners. These people just don't have any extra money at all to spend.

Another 6% buy according to price because they choose to. They can afford more but choose to stay with the lowest price "budget hotel" or shop at the discount stores in town. This is not to be confused with the person who is on a strict budget by necessity and must always search for the lowest price. The people that choose to purchase according to price without regard to quality or service are the most difficult buyers to please but are certainly easy to predict.

> *. . . less than 10% of the buying population makes purchasing decisions solely based on price.*

I've always had a "loss leader" in my store and

do so for the person who is looking for something inexpensive to buy. This only applies to 13% of the overall population in America. The rest can be "pulled up" by the retailer. That means that 87% of the people calling your store or walking into your store aren't primarily concerned with price. It's up to you how much they spend.

I was in the "pulling down" mode for almost twenty years and thought that I had to be like Wal-Mart. When you see a successful retailer like Wal-Mart, as a business owner you might be tempted to assume that they have the pattern you should follow. I was always trying to keep my price, so it matched what Wal-Mart or Kmart did. I finally learned better.

We should copy or adapt some of the strategies that they use, but we do not want to look like them. We want our business to look like us and what works for our customers. For years we saw Wal-Mart run ads about "falling prices." That little, yellow, round, smiley face would fly around the store cutting prices with a sword while trying to convince you that it did it all for you. Retailers have operated for years under the assumption that the lowest price catches the most customers.

A few years ago, all of that abruptly changed. They went to a "neighborhood" theme. Now, with the economy in the tank, they have brought back a version of the "rollback pricing" and combined it with the neighborhood theme. They have realized that they were going after the "price shoppers" (13% of the economy) and decided to change course to "relationship building" instead. They and their massive in-house marketing team are smart enough to research, read the data, and apply it to their marketing efforts.

Once a year I visit a Wal-Mart. The prices are good, but I choose not to shop there for a different reason. I don't like long lines and anytime I am there it seems that I'm always in line for a long time.

I've noticed that Wal-Mart likes customers who pay with a check. They scan the check and give it back to you with a receipt. They now have access to your information from your payment method. They are in the information gathering business, and you should be as well.

Now that you've determined the habits of the consumer and the money side let's look at the actual sale. Take for example a hair salon that we will call The Hair Factory. Let's say Mrs. Smith has been coming into the salon for once a month for the past ten years. By looking at your records you can determine a lot about Mrs. Smith.

You will see she prefers Monday afternoons around 3:00. You can see that she gets her hair cut every month and gets a perm or other stylized hair treatments every three months. By keeping records and paying attention to them, you know her buying habit (every month) and her spending pattern ($28 every month and every three months a special hair treatment at $75).

It is your job as the chief marketing officer to see that Mrs. Smith stays within those parameters and attempt to pull her up if you are able. Mrs. Smith might already be at the upper-end tier of your business so now your job is to keep her happy and get referrals from her with a payment reward system in place to make her want to do this.

The LCV (lifetime client value) of Mrs. Smith is over $6,000, so you certainly don't want to lose her. By not staying in front of her, you risk her being "fished out" of your pond to someone else, thus allowing a theft of $6,000. This valuable client can be forever protected simply by keeping your eye on the ball (or fish).

When I lose any customer (especially a top tier one) I find out why and then try to make sure it doesn't happen again. I have lost a few over the years seemingly without reason, but over 95% have been because of my lack of effort and planning. If you see Mrs. Smith as a $6,000 customer instead of a $28 customer, you will look at her very differently. Her loyalty to you is valuable and should be appreciated and rewarded.

There are a number of things that you can do to insure she remains a loyal customer. The first thing you must do is pay attention to the details of Mrs. Smith. As you value, appreciate, and continue to cultivate her loyalty, she becomes a "funnel" for new customers. A happy, valued customer creates referrals, and referrals mean no customer acquisition cost to you. When you start to get those, it's time to shout Hallelujah!

> *A happy, valued customer creates referrals . . .*

Perhaps this sounds automatic to you, but it's very easy with a store full of people and hundreds of other customers to let this get by you. You should have a chart or at least some account notes that document the buying habits and spending patterns of your customers. If you see those patterns changing you can know there's a problem and you can catch it before someone else "catches" her.

In my florist business I have three groups of customers. I think this holds true for most of the small-business world. I have customers who buy on a regular basis. I know all about them and their families and I've determined their habits so that I can spend my energy pulling them up the buying scale.

The next group is those who buy a few times a year but are not in the top 20% of my customers in terms of spending. With these customers I spend my energy to pull them up into the upper part of the "customer triangle" and get them to buy more frequently and to spend more.

Lastly, there are those customers who aren't loyal to me at all. They shop the yellow pages or other directory guides (which I hate) and buy very randomly. I used to never pay much attention to this group until one day while taking an order I asked the gentleman, "Have you ever purchased from us before?" He said he did not think so but when I entered his name, he had. The buying history of his account was that he would buy for a year or so and then fall off the face of the earth for a few years.

We have five years of data in our main system, so I asked him about it. He stated that he and his wife moved around a lot and he would end up back here every few years. He then said, "I would have kept using you guys if I knew who you were and how to contact you." This was a clear "business failure" on my part!

You might say, "Rick, what's the big deal?" but his average ticket item was $100. So that means he's an "A customer" and will potentially buy three to five times a year. That puts his worth to me at $6,000. I let him slip through the non-existent filter that should have been in place.

After taking his order and giving him a "welcome back, Rick's a dummy discount" I got all the information I could get from him (with the exception of his underwear size) and you can rest assured this store will keep him informed.

There's a lot to learn by just asking customers for their information. Remember, there's value in talking to your customers. I now have an employee who monitors the "fallen by the wayside" accounts. We mail to them twice a year and we get some back or re-connected with us. That is making us money and taking it from a competitor.

Now, let's say two months go by and we don't see Mrs. Smith. Unless Mrs. Smith just lost all her money in the stock market there's a good possibility that she has wandered away.

While in the midst of writing this chapter, one of my designers said to me, "I haven't seen Mrs. Smith in a while." I quickly looked at her records and here's what I found: she is a top 25 customer, so we see her or hear from her on the phone three to four times per month. Immediately I dropped a card in the mail saying "we've missed you" from all the gang at A Floral Boutique Florist. If I don't hear back, I give them a call.

A top-tier customer is worth the effort to keep them coming back. A card, phone call, free flowers, or other gift is worth it to you and it ultimately saves you money. If you had to go out and get another Mrs. Smith it could cost you hundreds of dollars.

In our case, Mrs. Smith was elderly, had had a fall and had been in a rehab. She was now home. None of us were aware of this. She called the day after receiving the card and told us her story. We immediately sent her get well flowers and a note telling her not to hesitate to call us if we could help. This is the way you keep your best customers.

Good deeds come back to you . . .

I've had drivers show up at people's doors and do all sorts of things to help them. One day we delivered food for a lady who was just caught in a jam with time. No, I didn't charge her either. Good deeds come back to you and sometimes even in dollar signs.

Chapter 5
Just Ask

Once you've gotten the customer into a proper funnel and you know all that there is to know, then it's time to put that customer to work for you. Your database can be your best employee—it is never late to work or asks to go home early.

Let's take Mrs. Smith from the salon that we discussed before. Once she's in her slot and we know why and how often she is there, then we can become a trusted friend of hers. When someone trusts you in a business relationship they will work very hard for you because they believe in what you do. Some of my biggest events come from out of the blue from my customers. I run at least one "customer referral" campaign a year and I believe in rewarding people who send me new accounts. I reward for not just a name and a phone number, but a true sale.

Recently I obtained a new customer whose first purchase was larger than the average account for a florist.

That amount (because of previous research)

showed me that if someone spends this amount, there's more to get. While entering the information into the computer, I asked her what florist she had previously been using.

She did not offer a name but said that repeatedly they would call "their florist" and no one there would know who they were and what they ordered as the "usual piece" for their employees. After years of being treated this way they were ready for a change. Numerous people (customers and employees) told her how good our work was. Then, one day, they received one of our promo pieces and decided to use us for a large party.

After the party, I called to ask how everything was. I then told her that we would love to have her ongoing business and asked if we could do anything else for her. Her reply was, "Yes, you can" and she gave us all of their business. They are a $5,000 a year account ($60,000 LCV customer) who my competitor allowed to be fished out of their pond.

So many businesses don't ask for help from their customers because of a fear of offending them. I've been told countless times "Just ask."

You should have a system in place where customers are rewarded for the referrals that they give you. For years, I did not believe in paying for referrals, but I changed my mind when I learned in my marketing group that paying for good strong leads or customers is cheaper in the long run. The average cost for a new customer could range from $50 to $100 or even higher. If your business is on a 10% net profit bottom line, then that customer would have to spend $500 or better before you make any money.

So, if a customer calls and gives you a lead and you pursue it and that results in a new customer, then all the money they spend allows you to make a profit from the first order. You then have the money to put into customer service and can truly service your accounts and give your customers some items that your competitors can't.

You . . . need to make sure that all your customers are aware of how much you appreciate their business.

I reward customers with a discount on their account along with a thank-you card from me. I make sure I handwrite it and sign it. I always thank them for allowing me to be their "florist of choice." You, as the business owner, need to make sure that all your customers are aware of how much you appreciate their business and that you are in charge of customer relations.

In today's economy there are so many choices, and the "big guys" know how to go after your customers and capitalize on them. You and I have something that they can't offer—personal service. Your customers can have the name and phone number of a local person who they can talk to, and if marketed right, they will spread the word for you. Who really likes doing business with someone they don't know? The small-business owner is in the driver's seat in this area.

In the late 1990s, the big box guys took over in many business arenas, but lately times are changing, and the pendulum is swinging back to small-business owners. In these days of "press five for more information," people are switching back to smaller companies at record numbers.

In the current economy, people want the personal relationship and do not want to talk to machines. In the earlier chapter I spoke about how effective robo-calls are and that's true, but only if the person you're calling knows you and has a good relationship with you.

The big box guys are very good at marketing. They have the money to attract the best employees with the best talents that money can buy. But small-business owners have something in their arsenal that the big box will never have: the ability to relate to the customer and the needs of the customer.

I engage ALL of my customers when they call with something that will connect us. I can talk about politics, religion, kids, hobbies, etc. Some people are used to dealing with a big box and just don't like "getting personal" with people. They would rather deal with machines or operators they don't know. Don't even try to win this group over because you won't get anywhere. They might, after some time, get tired of big box and maybe they will come to you at that point. I estimate this segment to be less than 5% of the market, so I wouldn't spend time worrying about it.

Another form of "just ask" is a reminder service. If you have a retail business that depends on people knowing or being reminded of special occasions, then here is another opportunity for you to reap in the sales.

Today, people are so busy that they need all the help they can get. If you have a gift store or other retail store, then start gathering information for your database along with the dates of importance. Then, develop a plan to let them know of the impending occasion. You'll be surprised at how many people will respond to your request if they know that your intentions are to help them to not look bad.

Customers DO NOT mind being reminded of events or occasions even if a sales pitch is attached. One recent month I ran a survey and asked customers who called several questions regarding this topic. Almost 85% said they did not mind being solicited for something as long as they were familiar with the event/occasion.

In my field, florists are leaving thousands of dollars on the table every year by not aggressively using reminders as a marketing tool. It seems to me that using this tool is relatively rare in most industries.

About every three months, I get a cold call from a national monitoring service (an alarm company). They go through their sales pitch and at the end they say, "If you refer us today to three friends of your business we will take off 10% of the yearlong price." All of this is just asking. It's cheaper for them to give me a 10% discount than to keep the woman on the phone doing cold calls. These types of calls are very ugly and can leave a bad taste in the mouth of customers. I will never do a cold call, it's way too risky.

Another form of "just ask" is to solicit partners to help you. As I mentioned before, I love working with Outback Steakhouse. I partner with them at every holiday and I add an Outback gift certificate into some of my billings in exchange for discounts and free Bloomin' Onions. Who doesn't like a free bloom?

When the hit movie Valentine's Day came out, I partnered with our local Regal Cinemas to do a big campaign for the release of this movie on Valentine's Day 2010. We collected names, addresses, and emails raffle-style in a large bowl. Through the campaign we gained over 100 new accounts! We began to include them in our "marketing funnel" and saw results within thirty days.

I often ask businesses to partner and do joint mailings or marketing campaigns. I am often declined, but occasionally I will stumble upon a partnership that really works. They don't have to be in the same field or even directly related to my business. I once allowed a pest control company to advertise in our mailings. I found out a month later that he got about ten new customers from the mailing and they used him because of the relationship they have with us.

You have to know the person you are partnering with, be confident in the quality of their work, and trust them implicitly. One thing is for sure, however, NEVER GIVE THEM A COPY OF YOUR LIST! Always guard your list and never allow anyone to fish your list. You do the fishing and allow them to bait your pole.

Chapter 6
Lifetime Client Value

When I first heard the term "Lifetime Client Value" (LCV) I didn't know what it was referring to. After learning about LCV and finally placing it into my business model, I realized quickly that I had been looking at customers the wrong way. I, like most business owners, had always been looking for the new customer. I would spend hundreds or even thousands of dollars and never get the account that I was pursuing.

Amazingly, every advertiser who comes through my door tries to convince me that customers will magically appear if I just run one ad with them. This is obviously untrue, and what's more, you will spend a small fortune doing this. Ask the advertisers why THEY don't advertise.

Growing your customer base and making more money comes down to expanding your customer base, getting them to spend more money, and more frequently.

This sounds so easy but very few do this. Instead, they sit back and take the business that comes their way and then grow satisfied with making 3% to 5%.

When I look around at other businesses I see some people really making money, but the majority are just getting by. When you really examine what you see, you will find out that the people who are making good money are doing so because they have developed a relationship with their customers and have made it their goal to try to increase the frequency of the buy.

In my last book, I discussed the concept that the owner's main job is that of pulling customers up the "customer triangle" (see diagram on page 61). You can invariably divide your customer base into A customers, B customers, and C customers. The C customers are on the bottom of the triangle, B in the middle, and the A's are on top. Your sole job as the owner or manager of your business is to pull that customer up the triangle. If you can pull a low-level customer up to a mid-level customer, then the LCV of that person could double or triple.

One example of this is if you have a C customer who buys from you six times a year and spends about $50 per visit; they have a $300 value per year. If the average customer length for your industry is twelve years, then the worth of that customer is $3,600. The later number gets your attention more than the first number.

If, through some of the means we've

discussed in this book (chapter 2), you can pull him or her into the next highest level (B), then that group might be a customer who buys from you twelve times per year at $50 each time. That customer can be valued at $600 per year or $7,200 over a lifetime. Trust me when I say that it will cost you a lot less to pull him or her up than to spend the thousands that it will take to get new customers who will spend that kind of money with you.

CUSTOMER TRIANGLE

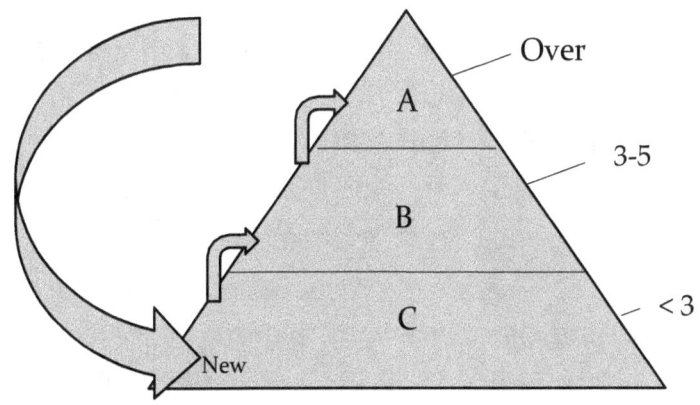

Most of your customers will be in one of the above brackets. Your job is to pull each customer up one level. If you are doing the marketing correctly, then the upper tier of the triangle will bring you new customers who will start at the bottom tier. Thus, the cycle continues until your top 5% brings in closer to 25% of your orders. What comes from that is "abundant profit."

It might be as simple as offering a rewards program, as easy as a follow-up phone call or comment card, or as effortless as just plain asking for more business. Business owners have not been placing a value on their customers and are just now starting to realize what a customer is truly worth.

> . . . a customer who buys from you four to eight times a year is a gold mine . . .

Big box has known for years that a customer who buys from you four to eight times a year is a gold mine for you. Now all you have to do is "fish in your own pond." If all of your marketing is working right, you will almost never have to spend any more money on new customer acquisitions because your A's will hand you all your new C's on a platter. Then the whole process starts all over again.

For years advertisers would come into my store and place me with everyone else competing for the same customers. A national wedding vendor, for example, has been relentless at trying to get me to advertise or market with them. Eventually, I asked their representative, "Why would I want to be thrown into a group with all these people advertising for the same thing I am? Wouldn't I catch more customers in my own pond?" She just looked at me speechless.

What they are doing is creating a pond (as we talked about earlier) and then getting everyone to buy a pole (advertise) and fish in their pond. So, you have 100 vendors that want more customers and we're all standing around the pond with our poles in the water trying to catch the same fish.

Sometimes the fishermen outnumber the fish in the pond. Your chances of catching a fish are a lot less than if you were there all by yourself. Even if you didn't catch as many fish your attempts would be more profitable. In business today, the time demands are growing rapidly, so our time must be managed in all areas, including advertising and marketing.

Another reason to establish the LCV of your customers is to determine the customers who aren't worth having. I know most people don't want to talk about it but there are customers who aren't profitable to have. The customer who complains the most, for example, probably is not the best customer you have.

> *. . . there are customers who aren't profitable to have.*

My favorite show is Kitchen Nightmares with Chef Gordon Ramsey. Just like Chef Ramsey, every now and then you need to tell somebody the truth and tell them to piss off. When I did my business makeover a few years ago I discovered early on that who I thought were my best customers were actually not.

You've heard me say that only 13% of the buying public has to buy by price. It was that group that was getting all my attention and I wasn't even making money on them. I decided to raise my prices by 28% over the course of a year and that weeded out some of them.

A few of them were pulled up in the triangle and now are good customers of our store. They are now working for us, getting us new customers over and over. You have to face the truth that sometimes not all customers are good to have.

If you have a customer who has a buying pattern of once a year and spends $30 and this pattern lasts for years, there's a pretty good chance that the customer might not be worth spending energy and money on. I look at customers like the Bible, if your faith isn't growing, then you are going backward.

With today's economic trends you really need to sharpen your skills when it comes to marketing.

With today's economic trends you really need to sharpen your skills when it comes to marketing. I see people who are on target and making good money and those who are on target by accident and have no clue where the business comes from. Take American Express for example.

I've been a member for thirty years and

there's never been a time that I didn't get the best service that can be offered. They hit me with directional pieces, emails, and phone calls and they keep me using their card. On several occasions over the last few years, I've needed to dispute a charge and they don't even hesitate. They take it off and make the merchant justify why they should put it back. I've won all three times and always get a follow-up call as to how it was handled. American Express has perfected customer service in my case, and for that reason I remain loyal.

Chapter 7
Don't Play Follow-the-Leader

Car salesmen are a great example of what I mean when I say, "Don't play follow-the-leader." I have a favorite salesman who works at a large dealership in my town and over the years I've bought at least ten cars from him. He has always kept in touch with me and lets me know what's going on and when to buy.

Every time I pull into the dealership I have to laugh at what I see. As I turn the corner and enter the lot, the salesmen are lined up outside, some smoking, some drinking coffee, or on their cell phones. The golf carts are lined up like the start of the Daytona 500 just waiting for the green flag to drop.

As my vehicle nears, they all look up and start looking back and forth at each other. All of them are trying to size the car up before anyone gets out. They are trying to see if you're fair game or if you "belong" to someone.

They begin to ask each other: Is he kicking tires? Do you know him? Do you think he's here to buy a new or used? Once you get out and start walking their way, all of them put on their "happy face." Shirts get tucked in a little better and their A game begins.

The first thing you encounter is the handful of howdy. The grins and greetings begin and continue all the way down the line. After I get my jollies from the introductions, I mention my salesman's name. They hang their heads and say, "He's inside."

It wasn't until I became an expert in marketing that I realized how my favorite car salesman had mastered the art of marketing car sales. He does not have to go out and stand in the heat or cold looking for new customers. He has his own pond to fish in. Every day he throws his pole into his pond and spends thirty minutes keeping himself close to his customers. He fishes from the comfort of his office. He has an assistant whose sole job is to help him fish the pond.

As I discussed in earlier chapters, he has a well-stocked pond from all the years in business and he found the value of communication early on. He knew that by standing outside like the rest of the guys, he was not distinguishing himself from the crowd. So, he decided early on to distance himself from the other guys.

When I walked inside, the few salesmen inside "cooling off" did the same thing as the outside guys. Usually my guy was waiting at the counter and he also knew I was coming. I can remember one time having to wait three hours to get in to see him.

I would start getting calls from him after my vehicle was about two years old because he had determined my buying habits and when I would be the most likely to buy a new car. He also kept in touch with me yearly and wanted to know the birthdays of my children. Guess where we bought both cars when my kids started driving.

The reason for this chapter is to show you that you don't have to play follow-the-leader; not to pick on car salesman. But, you see how one guy did it differently and he had great results.

The car salesman (or most employees) only copy what they see. If all the salesmen come in and then all go outside and wait for the people to come to them, then that's all they know to do.

Once they get a customer they are only concerned with today's sale and not the LCV of the client in front of them. My guy knew back in 1980 that I would have to buy a car every two to three years, so he knew when to call. He knew my wife would need a new car every few years also, and when my children came of age he was right on the ball.

So many of us in business play follow-the-leader and do it only because we see others doing it. Marketing results are determined by how well you know your customer and their habits.

All of us have industry conventions that we can attend, and you will learn some excellent things. But usually they teach all of us the same things, so you have hundreds of florists, hair designers, car salespeople, tool salespeople, real estate salespeople, and so on all learning the same thing. It wasn't until I joined a national marketing group that I truly learned what marketing is. I now look at what I've learned and how to apply it in a new way. Some of these big box guys spend thousands on campaigns that would serve as great "crossover campaigns" for others' businesses.

I mentioned industry conventions earlier, but you have to also be careful. They tend to be geared toward the company that is hosting them. They bring in speakers that benefit their products or represent their beliefs and interests. You will learn something as long as you can keep the dynamics

Marketing results are determined by how well you know your customer...

in mind. If the presenter is speaking about social networking, at the end he will probably introduce you to a program that the host has in place. Let's face it, all programs are designed to benefit the host company. But you can learn from the content of the program and decide later how it will fit your needs.

Recently I met a friend from church who introduced me to a new program called "opt in text marketing." The concept is very simple: people can opt in to your "text network" and then you can send them specials, discounts, or messages anytime you like. The program allows them to voluntarily opt in or out with the sending of one message, so the customer has control. Consumers love when they have control of the access.

This program is working in restaurants but really didn't fit my business, or so I thought. It was designed for fast-food chains at first and then rolled out to other businesses. The concept came from the American Idol type shows where people are asked to vote with text. I believe this marketing tool will have longevity, but as always, something new will be along before too long.

Once someone starts this type of program, others will soon follow suit, so you will have to always be creative in the use of it. We have found that the program will work well during peak times, so you have to know when and where something will work for your business.

Do you spend any time at all keeping in contact with your customers? I never did until about three years ago, and when I did start what a difference it made in our sales numbers and profits. I always thought I had to make more sales in order to make more money. Now I understand that profit return should be the first priority. You might be scratching your head in confusion. Let me explain it this way.

I want my store to make a 10% bottom line after all expenses (including reasonable salaries for owners). By knowing this, I can build my sales numbers around it. At Valentine's Day, one of the biggest days of the year in retail and in my flower business, I would always set prices based on what I thought the competitor was going to do. I would even have the clerks call and find out the competing prices. I would then lay out my pricing plan, with profit not being first in the equation.

Now, I set up my profit points, determine pricing, and then see how much marketing it will take to achieve the profit projections. Trust me, this will make a huge difference in your business once you get this concept down and not vary from it. It was one of the hardest things that I've had to do.

My suggestion is that you pick the slowest day of the week to do this. Spend some time studying the numbers and patterns of your customers' habits. In my business, I go by dates of purchases and when I see a pattern three times in a row, then I have a really good chance of selling that customer.

Most men purchase the day of an event (anniversary, birthday, etc.) so it makes no sense at all to market them until the day before. When you get their attention by the date, then you can get a sale. I've hit as high as 29.6% on some weeks and I fully expect to hit even higher numbers as I tweak this system.

When I need to get away, I hitch up the boat and head for the river. I'll pick up dinner and head north on the river until I find a nice place to anchor. I put my cell phone on vibrate and pull out a pad and begin to write. *Do you spend any time at all keeping in contact with your customers?* If you get somewhere very peaceful and get your mind in check, then you can let the creative juices flow. You can write several campaigns and get a lot of future work done.

I start each year off by writing down on my legal pad the dates of all my campaigns and what I plan to do. I also include in that plan all my billings. The reason I do this is because if you bill or send out statements twenty-six times per year then you need twenty-six campaigns. You're allowed by the post office to have 2.82 ounces of mail in the envelope for first class mail, and you should fill it to the max.

One of the best examples of a business that uses this concept is the Flower Shop Network. They are a floral network company that sends and receives orders. When I get a check from them and open the envelope, three to five pieces of marketing information are included. They are all industry related, and I've used several of the vendors in my flower shop.

I have allowed other businesses outside my industry do this in my mailings. I've taken as little as $50 for allowing a local restaurant to market in my mailings. During the major holidays or events in your business, you'll be surprised at who will pay you to be included in your billings.

One concept that temporarily got my attention was video messaging. This concept started almost ten years ago in a restaurant here in the Daytona area. I was asked to be the first advertiser. I felt so privileged then to be included. Now, of course, I would tell them to piss off.

The concept was that a company installed a large, flat-screen TV in the restaurant and then did ads that cycled every five to seven minutes. You could change the ad if you wanted but you would have to pay a $35 fee. I did the program for five months and made one change per month. The monthly cost was $49 (which I thought reasonable) and with the one change a month it came out to be $84 a month. Based on what I know now I would have had to do $840 per month to break even on my investment and anything over that would have been profit.

I log all calls, and have for years, on how people heard about us. The most calls that I received in a month from the video messaging program during the five months that I participated was

If you can't measure it, then you are playing craps with your money . . .

twelve. So, based on that number I was losing almost half of my money. One competitor friend of mine did it for five years and every time I would ask him how it's going he would say "great" but offered no way to measure his results. If you can't measure it, then you are playing craps with your money and betting the whole stack of chips on someone else's agenda.

While on our Sunday drive this week, my wife and I stopped at one of our country restaurants and when I looked up I saw a brand-new flat-screen running ads, a mug with the same ads, and the place mats matched also. I know they were paying over $100 for this per month. I watched all the videos and one hour after eating breakfast couldn't remember one advertiser on the display. Either it's not real effective or my memory is leaving me.

If you haven't guessed by now, I love to eat at the Outback Steakhouse in my hometown of Ormond Beach. Both the former proprietor and the current one are friends of mine. When my son wanted a part-time job and asked my advice for a job during college, without hesitation I said Outback Steakhouse. He asked why, and I told him that as much as I eat there, I've always seen a fine-oiled machine at work. They know how to treat their customers and have realized long ago the LCV of their customers.

My son applied for and got a job. He started out as a bus person and then was given the opportunity to move up. He became a server and realized that what I had told him was true. He realized that he could have a career in the company if he wanted. He later transferred to one of the busiest Outback Steakhouses in the country, and when we would go there to eat, everything was the same despite how busy they were.

My daughter took the same path with the restaurant Maggiano's. It's a fine-dining Italian restaurant in Orlando that serves family style in a huge dining room. They, like Outback, also realized the importance of customers and the value that they bring to their establishment. My table was visited all the time by servers, management, and other staff. I've never felt "abandoned" by either chain. Neither of these chains plays follow-the-leader. They play we-are-the-leader-follow-us.

Chapter 8
Bring Back the Salesman

It was when I heard Gene Simmons of Kiss say something in a speech once that really made me stop and think about my business. He said that there are very few salesmen left in the country. We've gone to being "order takers" and not salespeople. The order takers do a good job but only sell what they have a package for at pre-determined prices. The true salesperson really spends time evaluating the customers' needs and developing a package just for them.

A good salesperson doesn't talk about price at all. How can you give someone a price if you don't know what their needs are? We might think we know what their needs are, but do we really? This is the hardest of things to teach someone in sales. Everyone wants to jump to price first, when price (in retail) is really down to three or four on the list.

As I have said a number of times, only 13% of America buys by price. That number drove me crazy for a long time until I found that my data matched that number also. That means the rest of the buying public is in your hands, waiting to be molded into need versus price.

At my retail flower shop we got away from discussing price until the very end of the sale. Sometimes we would even close sales without talking price and this was one of the hardest things to teach salespeople. If customers have in their mind what you are selling them, then they are pretty close on price.

...the buying public is in your hands, waiting to be molded into need versus price.

The price and the sale in our store match almost every time. Yes, there are some times when people are thinking big and showy but the money they want to spend is not in line with the purchase, so you do have to deal with that scenario.

In the old days for us, when someone would call the flower shop we would cordially greet and ask how we can assist them. As soon as someone says, "I want to send flowers," everyone was trained to say, "And what would you like to spend?" The customer would either say a price or ask what the minimum was. We would then get into what I call a "money yo-yo." We would go back and forth, and we would leave money on the table, but it was our fault.

After learning what true sales are we

changed our format. After the greeting, we now say, "Tell us a little about the occasion you are purchasing for." They explain the occasion—birthday, anniversary, etc.—and after a minute or two the "sale" can begin.

The sale would not start until after the clerk and the customer both felt comfortable with each other and the words "may we take your order." Remember, people like to be asked for their business and once they agree then they give the "price power" to you. You've successfully taken the "money yo-yo" out of the equation and made the rest of your job easier.

We go through all the information on the order and still not mention price. The price is left for the very last when we ask for a form of payment. Some customers will ask, "What is my total?" and with confidence the clerk will reply.

Our clerks are trained to "let it roll" if not asked and simply give a total after adding fees and taxes. You can tell by the sound of their voice if you've broken the "price windshield" for them. If you did *The price is* break that bank you can simply *left for the* adjust back or explain in more *very last . . .* detail the value that is there.

In 99% of the times that the customers objected (which is very few) it was my fault for not giving the perceived value versus price. During the initial conversation you have time to pull up their account and see all their history in front of you. While writing this chapter I spoke to an A customer one day and when I pulled up her account, I noticed she spends a lot of money on close relatives but not on friends or others. If I had not been able to see this information, then I wouldn't have known how to "sell" to her or I would have undersold her. You have to be able to access the sales information.

One area we don't do is "add-on sales." They are the ugly cousin of sales. If the add-on needed to be part of the original sale, then why wasn't it? Many trades people say, "Add-on sales are where it's at." I would agree with that in the fast-food industry, but in retail it sounds so tacky and it should be part of the "sales process." Take this line out of your business model and be more creative on sales.

One year during Valentine's Day my wife suggested that balloons just be part of our three sales levels. So, when we did our prototypes, we did. After the holiday passed, we had increased Valentine's Day balloon sales by 20%. Wow!

So, the next year we added chocolates and sales went up again. Finally, we offered a special that had chocolates AND balloons. It's an item that we charge $199 for and have no problem getting it.

Before being creative, we would sell roses for $99 and attempt to add on the items. Not everyone wants to buy balloons and chocolates, so we create other specials for those who don't want the all-inclusive.

One place where I used to get my hair cut would push add-on items to the point where I got tired of going there. How's that for an add-on sale? They've lost a customer for life now and if they know anything about LCV then they have just lost over $5,000 from me. So, if it's not meant to be part of the original sale, then why try to add it on? Your customer will appreciate you for not doing it.

In the floral business you always have to deal with funerals. The loss of a loved one, whether expected or not, is devastating. Usually after the funeral home, the florist is the next place families visit. I would see cars pull up full of people and I knew it was either a funeral or the Jehovah's Witnesses stopping by to say hi.

After listening to what they have in mind, we would have to determine the money level that they would need to accomplish what they were looking for. Most buyers have in mind what they want, but we don't do a very good job at extracting that from them. We are hoping they will make it easy and just tell us, but most situations don't work out that way.

I remember one example when my daughter

told me she was going to book a "simple funeral." When I looked over she was sitting with five people. They were very emotional, and I knew it would take her a while. After about thirty minutes, I walked over, and they had not even got past who, what, when, where, and how.

About an hour later, Jessy was finally done. She thanked the family and they left. She proceeded to enter the orders and the funeral topped $2,000. This was a large funeral by any store's standard. They had told Jessy on the phone that it would be a simple funeral, but when they got here, and Jessy began to "sell" as she was trained to do, they began to see what they needed instead of allowing their wallets to control their buying habits. Remember, 80% plus do not have to buy by price.

When my wife takes me shopping, I love to sit and watch people and how they shop. While sitting in the mall one day, a couple sat on the bench next to me. They were discussing a purchase and promised each other that they would not buy because of pressure, only need.

About an hour later they walked out of the big box electronics store we were sitting in with a 52" LCD TV and the best DVD player in the store. I started to laugh out loud and as the wife walked by me she winked at me and said, "We need it."

So, it doesn't matter what you say prior to

shopping, this example proves that if you have the right salesman there's no telling what can happen. I know there are times when people are sold items that they don't need, but I think is a very small percentage.

Another example of this is the add-on plans for warranty. At the register they always ask, "Do you want to protect your purchase with an extended warranty plan?" This is what all big box people who sell you electronics are trained to do and say. I've heard that as many as 30% of people say yes to this. This alone proves how easy people can be moved. So, it's time for you to look at your business and see if you have salesmen employed, or just order takers.

Chapter 9
Get Out of My Pocket

This chapter deals with all the people who want to get into your pocket. Very few people who attempt to get into your pocket really provide a service or value to you. In every profession or business there are people who attempt to sell you on products that they have to pedal. It took me years to learn this concept: if someone brings something to you rather than you calling wanting to buy it, then it probably won't help you much.

Salespeople for years would come through the flower shop and present me with "the sales pitch." Sometimes I would say yes without doing the proper research. Then about three or four months later, I would realize that I had wasted my money.

My first example was some advertising done in a local church directory. One day I received a cold call from a major advertiser who was representing all the local Catholic churches in the area. They said that they were in need of a florist to advertise with them and that a package price could be done for all the churches if we could do all of them. After listening to the "recording" I jumped on this—and I want to use this example of how business owners are sold these types of items.

What made me jump on this were two things. First, the congregation that could be reached by advertising in this guide would be over 8,000 people, or so they said. So, the price of $900 spread out over the amount of people was really affordable and looked like it would make us money.

Second, the promise (with no written guarantee) of exclusivity was very attractive. They told us they could not prevent any other florist from advertising   in the guide, but they "would not seek" other flower shops and that with only three days left, we were the only store. We wrote the check (50%) and waited for the copy phase. We crafted a nice ad that would appeal to the members and waited to make money. Remember, neither Susie nor I went past a few years of college and have no formal business degree.

This concept is "promise and wait." and it will NEVER make you money.

When the copy came it was just our ad on a separate page. We made a few changes and then requested a second copy along with the entire ad page. (We were trying to be smart.) The second proof came, and the ad looked great and we even increased the size of the ad and paid MORE. Don't call me an idiot yet, there's more to come.

We finally got the first church guide in the mail after thirty days and looked to see our "great ad." The ad was there, looked great, but there were three other florists along with a nursery center. We were livid and started calling the advertiser and they reminded us that they couldn't promise exclusivity. Susie and I were beside ourselves. Even back then we tracked all our sales and, needless to say, we lost money on that deal.

When we receive a call like that today, we take all the information and then do our "due diligence." Had I simply looked at the last few directories, I could have seen that this guide was a service guide for the congregation, but a great majority of the people don't use this guide at all. If I had compared the most recent guide from one several years earlier, I would have seen that they go through a lot of advertisers. That's a strong indicator that the return on investment is not very good, otherwise businesses would stay with it.

> . . . as high as 80% of print media doesn't pay for itself.

We were only in for one year. Lessons like this are plentiful and painful. I've read that as high as 80% of print media doesn't pay for itself. It does offer new businesses a way to get their names out, but without an offer or a way to track, I think you're wasting your time and money.

Another area to really lose on is charities that call and ask for donations. We get hit hard with this. In our county there are over 400 licensed charitable organizations not including schools. Some of them will bring you business but you have to be able to track that.

I used to donate to so many events per month and then start saying no. We now pick ten charities to support and partner with them. Now we ask for a level of sponsorship (gold, silver, platinum, etc.) and then we ask that our basic costs be covered. Once you do this you weed out most charities. The food, alcohol, and other items aren't for free; they might be discounted but are not free.

We have several charities that we like to partner with and do so each year. We ask for a letter in writing in advance as to their needs and what would be in it for us. We then negotiate the terms and what our involvement will be along with an exclusivity agreement. If you act like a business, then you'll be treated like a business.

I've never documented a loss of sale from not being in an event.

I don't do marketing or advertising unless it has exclusivity in it. I'm not into doing what everyone else wants to do. One charity got angry with me one time and said, every florist in the county is giving us three free pieces, so why couldn't I do the same? Then they told me that my customers would be there and that I shouldn't miss them and let someone else take them. I had to chuckle.

I've never documented a loss of sale from not being in an event. I have, however, documented getting customers from events the way that we do them. This practice has bit me in the butt a few times and made some of my competitors not real happy with me. Oh well.

So, the main lesson in this chapter is to know who's in your pocket, how much they want, and whether it's worth it.

Last year I decided to remove our business ads from all yellow page directories. There are four yellow page companies in our area, and we are too small an area to have four companies like this. As each one would enter this market they would make an appointment and attempt to sell you on why you had to advertise with them and how they were going to gain market share. The main yellow pages in this area was, in my opinion, the only game in town; all the others were little players trying to piggyback in the market.

Three years ago, I began to really study and calculate the costs of ads and my return on investment. When I finally got all my numbers crunched, the facts showed that yellow page advertising was not profitable.

My yellow pages rep began to state her case and stated that people use the book very heavily in two areas: florists and pizza. When she was done, I told her that the pizza store or flower shop wasn't doing their job. If they had been, perhaps the person would have known about the business already without having to search the yellow pages.

She then replied, "What about new customers?" I told her that if a proper "referral system" was in place, then new customers should be plentiful. After about three or four of these rebuttals, she gave up.

My total yellow pages cost for four books went from $6,000 per year to about $1,000 per year. So, I had $5,000 more to use that could generate more sales with LCV's instead of speculation shoppers. I wasn't trying to save the money. The money was within our budgeted range, so we had this money to spend elsewhere.

There are numerous reasons why the yellow pages did not work for me. First of all, most people using the yellow pages are over fifty years of age. If you're younger than that you are finding your information through mobile devices or Internet searches.

Every time I would pick up a phone book one of my kids would look the number up and hand me their phone before I could even get to the right page. Maybe now's the time for you to move some of those advertising dollars so you can now track what your results are versus what you are spending, or as we call it "return on investment."

There are so many more ways to find customers and for your customers to find you. If you use a customer triangle method, then you have new customers coming in and increased levels in purchases. So, look around your business and see whose hand you feel in your pocket and pull it out of there for good!

Chapter 10
Good is Good Enough

It took me the longest time to grasp and implement the title of this chapter. I, like everyone else, would put a project on the board and then 75% of the time would never get it done. The reason why is because I was always waiting for the project to be just perfect or just right. I could always find several reasons why it wasn't ready for implementation.

You do not need to be perfect in order to implement, you just need to begin to take action. The truth of the matter is that this is one of the obstacles that will prevent you from making money. You will procrastinate (not by choice) and the deadline will get by for the holiday or event you were waiting on. I talk to florists every day who would try to market for the holidays and they miss it because of always thinking that what they have is not good enough. There are numerous products out there that have been introduced and then re-introduced many times.

One of my favorite companies that does this is McDonald's. They roll out sandwiches, test market the data, and then re-try them again several more times. Each time they change something that will make it better. In one seminar I heard that the Big Mac was rolled out several times before it became what it is now. The Big Mac is the biggest selling sandwich ever and nothing will ever come close to its sales numbers.

Good is good enough means that if you have a compelling message and offer then get it out to the people with what you have. Maintain good records as to how it performs; you can then tweak it for the years or campaigns to come. I don't think I've rolled out one project in the last few years that I didn't go back and "re-do" for the sake of the product or sales numbers.

Disney World is another favorite. When they first rolled out the eating plans or "menu plans" as they call it, people said that will never work. Now the all-inclusive packages are one of their biggest sellers. I get all the emails and informational items from them and they've changed the menu system several times, making it better and better each time. The perceived value always goes up with a price increase. With good sales numbers you can do this. Now the competitors are "copying" the concepts.

This year when Sea World opened the new water park Aquatica, they offered a monthly option to be directly debited from your account. They also had a food package for the visitors as they entered, and I was surprised at how many people bought. For $17.95 a day you could come and go as you pleased to a food pavilion and just show your arm band. One price and eat all day. I bought the package and went back all day and never paid for any meals, drinks, or desserts. Wow, what a deal! I would have spent that easily in a day and of course they did lose money on me.

As for the monthly debit, my son and daughter have season passes to all the parks and they simply debit their bank accounts $15 a month. Big box won't release their numbers, but I bet it's in the thousands.

One area where I see a lot of procrastination is in websites. All new businesses should have a website up and running the first day that they are open. Most often, however, they never go back later to make changes, updates, or tweak it for better results. Thousands of dollars are spent on web designs every year, with hundreds of web design companies out there. I get at least two or three calls a month from website companies and they can put a website up for you in twenty-four hours. We've really become a fast-food, fast-needing society.

Every business needs a way to communicate with its customers.

Another place that good is good enough is in

the area of communication. Every business needs a way to communicate with its customers. If you can't tell them what you sell, then you're not going to be in business very long.

When people I know go into business I usually get a phone call with an offer for a free lunch. At the lunch the people invariably ask me what the most important thing to do in their new business is and I invariably tell them, "Have a way to talk to your customers." I've had owners show me their plans and at the end I would ask, "Where is your plan for communication?" They usually just stare at me.

Have a way to talk to your customers.

Suddenly, they get their second wind and start showing me different forms of advertising. I explain to them that advertising is a one-sided form of communication. I ask about social media, texting, squeeze pages on the internet, etc. The next question I get is, "How do you communicate with YOUR customers?" That's when I explain my system.

So, now it's time for you examine your business and ask yourself a few questions. First, is there anything in my business that I can roll out that will create an "income stream?"

Second, are there any projects that have been sitting on the burner that can be quickly rolled out to generate income?

Third, can I buy into the statement that good is good enough and move forward with at least two marketing projects a month and put myself on a deadline?

You should have been able to answer at least two of these as yes and if you are in a service or retail business you should have said yes to all three.

My suggestion is that you get a legal pad and start with the first event that you want to market. Every small business has high and low seasons and there are plenty of people to market to.

After prioritizing, I would then construct a campaign and get it to the printer. I have a local printer but when I get an idea, the girl at the local Office Depot does a great job and is very efficient. One time I needed to catch a plane and forgot to have 100 disks shrink-wrapped. I went to her and told her I needed them in one hour and when I went back they were all done. Other times I've needed some quick copy change or other changes and she's been great for us. I've also used Office Depots in other cities and they never let me down.

You must have a good relationship with a regular printer because you will be printing more than what a "neighborhood" Office Depot can do for you. Always check the price. Sometimes they will surprise you in some areas.

After you've picked up from the printer, then get your list ready and on the top of the list have your goals written down as to what you're trying to accomplish with this mailing. I've even seen mailings that were more informative and have great results. I wish I knew your business so that I could help you more, but I think you're getting the picture.

During the mailing process, always send one to yourself so you can see if it stood out or not. Look at the mailing with some fresh eyes and try to see if you would be a buyer or do what the mailing is intended to do.

I have several people in my family who are or were in business, so I like to mail them (more as family than customers) and then get their feedback as to what they liked about it. I want to know if the message was clear and if it compelled them to buy. Then, before I do that mailing again, I tweak it to make it better each time that it goes out. If you do this you'll have a good understanding of good, and then good is good enough.

I hope you've enjoyed reading the book and invite you to visit either one of my websites, www.rickrivers.com or www.floristbootcamp.com and click on "leave my testimonial" to let me know what you think of the book and what helped you the most.

God bless.

Closing Thoughts

One of my teachers, who I adore, summed up what business life is really about: Success is about environment, schedule, and accountability. I'm on her personal Facebook and her fan page. She writes a lot about what takes the time of entrepreneurs and how to deal with it. So, in closing, I want to encourage you to look at the above statement and then deal with each area in the way that it applies to your business or needs.

Creating a good environment for yourself and your business sounds so easy but is really one of the hardest things to do. I have several groups that I meet with on a regular schedule and I've also gotten rid of numerous groups. The reason I did is because they might have been helping me grow as a person but were "stealing" valuable time from me that I could be using for the growth of my business ventures.

I'm not saying it's all about me, but you have to have a balance in each group that allows you to benefit. If it's one sided it's time to make a change. Also, a group where everyone benefits is a group that will feed off each other and your thoughts and ideas won't stay on the back burner because of other people's needs. So, basically, environment is who you surround yourself with and who you give your time to.

Next is schedule and it can mirror environment. You have to start managing your time better. I found this out the hard way by one day just being so exhausted that I spent three days in bed.

After attending my first Glazer Kennedy Insiders Circle Super Conference I heard one of the speakers talk about how "time vampires" can just suck the life out of you. I had never really looked at it like that before. I looked at my calendar and 75% of my meetings were the kind where people sat around and they discussed things, but never get much of anything done.

At the end of that meeting they would schedule another meeting. Wow, another meeting to accomplish nothing but setting another meeting. I quit all those meetings. Now I set some clear parameters, and if I am not accomplishing anything, I stop it cold in its tracks.

Another time vampire is your cell phone. I began dealing with two ladies who own a marketing group and in our first meeting they were on task. They had goals outlined for them and me. They then decided any future meetings would be done via phone appointments or email.

After the first few "phone appointments," I realized that this is what I had to do also. If someone is serious about you then they will comply. My cell phone is now being used less and less and my goal is to keep it that way. Remember your time can be sucked from you without you knowing it.

Last is accountability. I had never had anyone hold me accountable in business. I have a good friend who is a pastor and he and his wife hold my wife and I accountable spiritually. Why can't this be done in business also?

One of my local marketing groups began to do this for me several years ago. Once a month we would get together on a roundtable type presentation and then "discuss" our ideas and compare market research. We would then talk about how to apply it to our various industries.

Each month before we would leave we would have goals to get done in the next month. If we didn't reach or implement one of our goals, then the group would hold you accountable. The reasons were many, but in the end failure to implement usually was due to procrastination. So, if you have no one to hold you accountable, join a group that will help you.

Now it's time to take a hard look at your business and see where changes need to be made.

You've heard me throughout the book tell you the areas where I had to make changes and then how those changes made me more money or allowed me more time. Getting more time is valuable. Time allows you to do what you need or want to do. I welcome all comments to me at:

rrr32174@yahoo.com

About the Author

Rick Rivers was born and raised in Daytona Beach, Florida, and he currently resides in the adjacent city of Ormond Beach.

At the age of nineteen, Rick attended a job fair and accepted a job as a Daytona Beach Public Safety Officer. The face of Daytona was changing; city leaders were trying a new national program that consolidated the police and fire departments. This is where Rick met many friends and fellow officers. He worked both as a police officer and firefighter, performing duties that each field required. The program ended after a short time and Rick remained with the police department. The public safety program still exists in some smaller cities across the country and here locally.

During Rick's tenure, he encountered some life-changing situations and lost two very good friends. But it was the lessons learned in the police department that taught him the values that he has today. Rick served in various divisions of the police department.

During that time, Rick met and later married Susie LaTorre on July 18, 1981. Two beautiful children, Jessica and Jason, followed.

In 1985, Rick and Susie entered into the area of owning your own business and purchased a retail flower shop. A lot of things went right, and a lot also went wrong. Rick began to learn about marketing and advertising and the huge differences therein. Rick later left the police department after fifteen years of full- and part-time service to join the family business. During the years of the business, Rick, Susie, Jessica, and Jason all worked very hard in the business and learned a great deal from that experience. That is where we all learned what true customer service is.

In the late 1990s, Rick began to teach seminars on Holiday Planning and other areas of marketing. He even taught at one of the big three wire services conventions in Nashville, Tennessee. The economy has changed numerous times throughout the last twenty-five years and will continue to do the same. The Internet has played a big role in how business has changed. Advertising is becoming obsolete and marketing is the cream that is rising to the top.

In 2005, Rick joined a national marketing group that meets several times a year in various cities in the country. It is there where Rick and others sit in large and small groups to find out what's working and how to make it fit their businesses. Rick also ventured in a portable refrigeration business after ten years of being a former owner in a similar company.

Rick intends to become a business coach and teach fellow florists and other small-business owners. Rick has always believed that if you help others get what they want then you will always get what you want.

To order copies of this book and others by Rick Rivers, to purchase one of the many workshops on CD that are targeted for small business owners who want to take sales and marketing to the next level, and to find out where Rick Rivers will be speaking next, please visit:

www.floristbootcamp.com